481 USELESS FACTS
EVERY KID SHOULD KNOW

LOVE USELESS RANDOM FACTS?

THEN THIS IS THE BOOK FOR YOU.

ABOUT THE AUTHOR

EVAN J MALONE IS A FORMER TEACHER TURNED AUTHOR WHO RESIDES IN CHICAGO, IL.

HE HAS ENJOYED BOTH WRITING AND CREATING KIDS' BOOKS SINCE 2021. AS A FATHER TO 3 CHILDREN, HE BELIEVES EVERY KID SHOULD ENJOY READING, EITHER BY THEMSELVES OR WITH THEIR PARENTS.

EVAN IS HOPING TO RELEASE PLENTY OF BOOKS IN 2022 & BEYOND!

ARACHIBUTYROPHOBIA' IS THE FEAR OF
GETTING A PEANUT BAR STUCK
TO THE TOP OF YOUR MOUTH.

A BOLT OF LIGHTNING IS
AROUND FIVE TIMES HOTTER THAN THE SUN!

A CHAMELEON'S TONGUE IS USUALLY
LONGER THAN ITS BODY

CROCODILES ARE UNABLE TO STICK
THEIR TONGUES OUT!

ALL DOG'S NOSES ARE UNIQUE -
LIKE A HUMAN FINGERPRINT.

FOXES USE THEIR TAILS TO COMMUNICATE
WITH OTHER FOXES.

A GROUP OF FROGS IS CALLED AN ARMY.

HIPPO'S LIPS ARE ALMOST TWO FEET WIDE.

HIPPO'S CAN RUN FASTER THAN A MAN.

A JAR OF NUTELLA SELLS EVERY 2.5 SECONDS.

VIKING MEN ACTUALLY DYED THEIR HAIR BLONDE -
SOME EVEN DYING THEIR BEARDS TOO!

MALE OSTRICHES CAN ROAR LIKE A LION!

A NEUTRON STAR SPINS 600 TIMES
IN ONE SECOND.

PET HAMSTERS CAN RUN UP TO 8.5
MILES A NIGHT ON THEIR WHEELS.

A SHRIMP'S HEART IS LOCATED IN ITS HEAD.

A SHARKS BODY DOESN'T CONTAIN ANY BONES -
INSTEAD, ITS SKELETON IS MADE OF CARTILAGE.

LIKE ITS FUR, A TIGERS SKIN IS ALSO STRIPED

AROUND 70% OF AN ADULT
HUMANS' BODY IS WATER.

ABRAHAM LINCOLN - THE 16TH PRESIDENT OF
THE USA WAS ALSO A WRESTLING CHAMPION TOO!

ACCORDING TO GOOGLE, THERE ARE 129,864,880
UNIQUE BOOKS IN THE WORLD! THIS IS ONE OF THEM

THE AGE OF MOST STARS IS SOMEWHERE
BETWEEN 1 AND 10 BILLION YEARS OLD.

YOUR RIBS MOVE ABOUT 5 MILLION TIMES
A YEAR, EVERY TIME YOU BREATHE.

ALMONDS ARE ACTUALLY MEMBERS
OF THE PEACH FAMILY.

AN AVALANCHE HAS A TOP SPEED OF 80 MPH!

THE AVERAGE YAWN IS NEARLY
SIX SECONDS LONG!

AN OSTRICH'S EYES ARE BIGGER THAN
THEIR BRAINS.

ANCIENT EGYPTIANS WORSHIPPED
MORE THAN 2,000 DEITIES!.

ANCIENT GREEKS BELIEVED REDHEADS
BECOME VAMPIRES AFTER DEATH!

APPLES ARE ACTUALLY PART OF
THE ROSE FAMILY.

APPLES ARE ONE-QUARTER AIR. NO WONDER
THEY FLOAT IN WATER!

APPLESAUCE WAS THE FIRST FOOD
CONSUMED IN SPACE BY ASTRONAUTS.

AS WELL AS HAVING UNIQUE FINGERPRINTS,
HUMANS ALSO HAVE UNIQUE TONGUE PRINTS!

ASIA IS THE LARGEST CONTINENT ON EARTH.
IT HAS THE LARGEST POPULATION WITH
OVER 4.46 BILLION PEOPLE!

AUSTRALIA HAS OVER 750 REPTILE SPECIES -
THE MOST IN THE WORLD!

BABE RUTH WAS THE FIRST BASEBALL PLAYER
TO HIT A HOME RUN IN AN ALL-STAR GAME.
IT HAPPENED AT CHICAGO'S COMISKEY PARK IN 1933.

BEES CAN BE FOUND EVERYWHERE IN THE WORLD
- EXCEPT IN ANTARCTICA.

UP UNTIL 1913, IT WAS POSSIBLE FOR PARENTS TO MAIL THEIR KIDS THROUGH POSTAL SERVICES!!

IN THE 1960S, THE BEATLES TEAMED UP WITH AN INVENTOR TO CREATE THEIR OWN HEADPHONES. THEY WERE KNOWN AS "BEATLEPHONES."

IN THE UNITED KINGDOM, YOU ARE ABLE TO COMPETE IN AN UNDERWATER MOUNTAIN BIKE RACE!!

SOME CARS CAN ACTUALLY RUN ON USED FRENCH FRY OIL!

CATERPILLARS HAVE 12 EYES!!

PEANUTS ARE NOT NUTS!
THEY ARE PART OF THE LEGUMES FAMILY.

BLACK DEATH WIPED OUT 75 MILLION EUROPEANS,
OVER ONE-THIRD OF EUROPE'S POPULATION
AT THE TIME!

CASHEWS ACTUALLY GROW ON CASHEW APPLES.
THE FRUIT CONTAINS BITTER FLESH.

CATS ARE UNABLE TO TASTE ANYTHING
THAT IS SWEET.

CHING SHIH IS BELIEVED TO BE THE WORLD'S MOST
SUCCESSFUL PIRATE IN HISTORY. SHE WAS A WOMAN!

CLEOPATRA WAS QUEEN OF EGYPT FROM 50 TO 30 B.C.
SHE CAME INTO POWER AT 12 YEARS OLD AND
ACTUALLY MARRIED TWO OF HER BROTHERS
DURING HER REIGN.

CLOUDS APPEAR WHITE BECAUSE THEY ARE
REFLECTING SUNLIGHT FROM ABOVE THEM.

EARTH IS NOT SHAPED LIKE A PERFECT SPHERE!
IT BULGES OUT AT THE EQUATOR LOOKING
MORE LIKE A "SQUISHED BALL".

COOKIE MONSTER DOESN'T ACTUALLY EAT COOKIES ON
SESAME STREET - THEY'RE RICE CAKES!!

COWS ARE ABLE TO WALK UP THE STAIRS
BUT CAN'T GET DOWN!

CUBA AND NORTH KOREA ARE THE ONLY COUNTRIES
IN THE WORLD WHERE YOU ARE UNABLE
TO BUY OR SELL COCA-COLA.

DEER OFTEN FLASH THE WHITE UNDERSIDE OF THEIR TAIL TO WARN OTHERS ABOUT NEARBY DANGER.

IN ANCIENT ROME, THEY NOT ONLY HAD MALE GLADIATORS BUT ALSO FEMALE GLADIATORS!
A FEMALE GLADIATOR WAS CALLED A GLADIATRIX, OR GLADIATRICES.

BEFORE BECOMING THE 40TH AMERICAN PRESIDENT, RONALD WILSON REAGAN SERVED AS A LIFEGUARD AND SAVED AROUND 77 PEOPLE FROM DROWNING!

EASTER ISLAND HAS 887 GIANT HEAD STATUES THAT WERE CARVED NEARLY 2000 YEARS AGO?!?

ELEPHANTS ARE THE ONLY KNOWN ANIMALS
THAT CAN'T JUMP!

IF YOU COULD TRAVEL AT THE SPEED OF LIGHT,
YOU WOULD NEVER GET OLD!

IT IS IMPOSSIBLE TO LICK YOUR OWN ELBOW!

KETCHUP WAS ACTUALLY ONCE SOLD AS A MEDICINE.

MONKEYS CAN GO BALD IN OLD AGE,
JUST LIKE HUMANS.

NEPTUNE HAS THE FASTEST WINDS IN THE
SOLAR SYSTEM! ITS WINDS REACH SPEEDS OF UP
TO 1600 MPH!

ONE DAY ON VENUS IS ALMOST AS LONG
AS 8 MONTHS ON EARTH!

PEOPLE USED TO MAKE CLOTHES FROM FOOD SACKS
DURING THE GREAT DEPRESSION.

MONKEYS CAN GO BALD IN OLD AGE,
JUST LIKE HUMANS.

NEPTUNE HAS THE FASTEST WINDS IN THE
SOLAR SYSTEM! ITS WINDS REACH SPEEDS OF UP
TO 1600 MPH!

ONE DAY ON VENUS IS ALMOST AS LONG AS 8 MONTHS
ON EARTH!

PEOPLE USED TO MAKE CLOTHES FROM FOOD SACKS
DURING THE GREAT DEPRESSION.

PLUTO GOT ITS NAME FROM AN 11-YEAR-OLD GIRL, VENETIA BURNEY OF OXFORD!

RIPE CRANBERRIES CAN BOUNCE LIKE A BALL.

RUBBER BANDS ACTUALLY LAST LONGER WHEN THEY'RE REFRIGERATED?!

SEA OTTERS HOLD HANDS WHILE THEY SLEEP!
IT KEEPS THEM FROM FLOATING AWAY IN THE SEA.

SOME PERFUMES ACTUALLY HAVE
WHALE POOP IN THEM!

SOME SALAMANDERS CAN REGROW THEIR TAILS,
LEGS AND EVEN PARTS OF THEIR EYES!!

YOU CAN ESTIMATE THE TEMPERATURE OF A PLACE BY
THE NUMBER OF TIMES CRICKETS CHIRP IN A SECOND.

THE EIFFEL TOWER GROWS TALLER EVERY SUMMER
AND SHRINKS BACK IN WINTER!

THEATRE WAS INVENTED BY ANCIENT GREEKS!

THERE ARE ALMOST 2,000 THUNDERSTORMS
ON EARTH EVERY MINUTE.

YOU ARE AS TALL AS THE LENGTH OF YOUR ARMS
STRETCHED OUT.

YOU CAN BUY BOTH PYRAMID & SQUARE-SHAPED
WATERMELONS IN JAPAN!

THE FIRST LIVING CREATURE TO GO TO SPACE
WAS A DOG NAMED LAIKA.

DOGS ARE ABLE TO HEAR ALMOST 10 TIMES
BETTER THAN HUMANS!

DOLPHINS SHUT HALF THEIR BRAIN OFF WHEN
THEY SLEEP. THE OTHER HALF STAYS ALERT TO
PROTECT AGAINST PREDATORS.

DOGS CAN SMELL 100,000 TIMES BETTER
THAN HUMANS.

EMPEROR PENGUINS CAN STAY UNDERWATER FOR UPTO 27 MINUTES AND CAN ALSO DIVE UP TO 500M.

ALL THE BLOOD IN YOUR BODY PASSES THROUGH YOUR HEART EVERY MINUTE!

WITH EVERY STEP YOU TAKE, YOU USE 200 DIFFERENT MUSCLES IN THE BODY.

THERE WILL BE 9.7 BILLION PEOPLE ON EARTH BY 2050.

EYELASHES LIVE FOR ABOUT 150 DAYS
BEFORE FALLING OUT.

FINGERNAILS CAN GROW UP TO FOUR TIMES
FASTER THAN TOENAILS.

THE FIRST CANDY CANES HAD
NO STRIPES AT ALL.

THE NATIONAL ANTHEM OF GREECE
HAS 158 VERSES.

FRENCH FRIES ACTUALLY ORIGINATED
IN BELGIUM, NOT FRANCE.

FROGS DRINK WATER THROUGH THEIR SKIN.

GORILLAS BURP WHEN THEY ARE HAPPY!

THE FOOTPRINTS LEFT ON THE MOON WILL
LAST FOR 100 MILLION YEARS!

HAM THE ASTROCHIMP WAS THE FIRST
HOMINID IN SPACE!

THE LARGEST ACTIVE VOLCANO IN THE WORLD
IS HAWAII'S MAUNA LOA.

HAWAIIAN PIZZA WAS ACTUALLY INVENTED
IN CANADA!

HIPPOS PRODUCE PINK MILK.

HORSES AND COWS ACTUALLY
SLEEP STANDING UP.

HUMAN BLOOD TASTES AS SALTY
AS THE OCEAN.

HUMAN EYES ARE MADE UP OF NEARLY
2 MILLION WORKING PARTS.

THE HUMAN EYE CAN DETECT ABOUT 10 MILLION
DIFFERENT COLORS!

HUMANS ARE BORN WITH AROUND 300 BONES,
SOME FUSE TOGETHER AS WE GROW OLDER.
AS A RESULT, WE ONLY HAVE AROUND 206 LEFT
BY THE TIME WE BECOME ADULTS

HUMANS ARE THE ONLY ANIMALS WITH CHINS.

HUMANS NOT ONLY HAVE UNIQUE FINGERPRINTS BUT
ALSO UNIQUE TONGUE-PRINTS!

HUMANS SHARE 50% OF THEIR DNA WITH BANANAS.

HUMMINGBIRDS CAN FLY BACKWARDS.

ICE CREAM WAS ONCE CALLED "CREAM ICE."

IF YOU UNWRAPPED AN EGYPTIAN MUMMY,
ITS BANDAGES COULD STRETCH UP TO 1,600 METERS!

IN THE COURSE OF AN AVERAGE LIFETIME, YOU
WILL EAT AROUND 70 ASSORTED INSECTS
AND 10 SPIDERS WHILE SLEEPING.

THE ONLY SOURCE OF DIAMONDS TILL 1896
WAS FROM INDIA!

INSECTS HAVE BEEN AROUND FOR 350 MILLION YEARS.
TO PUT THAT IN PERSPECTIVE, HUMANS HAVE ONLY
BEEN AROUND FOR 13,000 YEARS.

AROUND 5% OF THE EARTH'S CRUST IS
MADE FROM IRON.

IT IS ILLEGAL TO STAND WITHIN 90 METERS
DISTANCE OF THE QUEEN WITHOUT SOCKS ON.

ON AVERAGE IT TAKES AROUND 50 LICKS
TO FINISH ONE SCOOP OF ICE CREAM.

A PINEAPPLE TAKES BETWEEN 2 & 3
YEARS TO GROW TO FULL SIZE.

IT TAKES EIGHT MINUTES AND 19 SECONDS FOR
LIGHT TO TRAVEL FROM THE SUN TO EARTH.

JUPITER COMPLETES A ROTATION AROUND ITS AXIS
IN JUST 10 HOURS - MAKING IT THE FASTEST
SPINNING PLANET IN THE SOLAR SYSTEM.

IT TOOK AROUND 1,500 YEARS TO
BUILD STONEHENGE.

YOU CAN'T WALK ON PLANETS LIKE JUPITER, NEPTUNE,
SATURN, OR URANUS, THEY DON'T HAVE A SOLID
SURFACE AND ARE MOSTLY MADE OF GAS.

IF YOU COULD DRIVE STRAIGHT UP, IT WOULD ONLY
TAKE 1 HOUR TO REACH SPACE.

IT WOULD TAKE 70,000 YEARS IN THE FASTEST
SPACESHIP TO REACH ALPHA CENTAURI - THAT'S
HOW FAR IT IS!

IT'S IMPOSSIBLE TO SNEEZE WITH YOUR EYES OPEN.

IT'S PHYSICALLY IMPOSSIBLE FOR PIGS TO LOOK UP INTO THE SKY!

KANGAROOS ARE UNABLE TO WALK BACKWARD.

MARS HAS LOWER GRAVITY THAN EARTH. THAT MEANS A PERSON THAT WEIGHS 200 POUNDS ON EARTH WOULD ONLY WEIGH 76 POUNDS ON MARS.

THE MAYANS WORSHIPPED TURKEYS AS GODS!

OVER 480 MILLION PEOPLE HAVE
PLAYED MONOPOLY.

MOST FISH DON'T HAVE EYELIDS.

MOST PENGUIN SPECIES ACTUALLY LIVE
IN WARM CLIMATES.

ALMOST ALL INSECTS HATCH FROM EGGS.

THE AVERAGE TIME FOR MOST PEOPLE
TO FALL ASLEEP IS 7 MINUTES.

MOST PEOPLE START LOOKING AT WEBSITES FROM
THE TOP LEFT CORNER. IT'S HOW WE'VE BEEN
TRAINED TO SEARCH FOR INFORMATION.

MYSTERY SNAILS CAN REGENERATE THEIR EYES
COMPLETELY AFTER AMPUTATION THROUGH
THEIR MID-EYESTALK!

ALMOST SIX MILLION JEWISH PEOPLE WERE
KILLED DURING WORLD WAR II.

ALMOST 10 PERCENT OF A CAT'S BONES
ARE IN ITS TAIL.

NEW ZEALAND ACTUALLY HAS MORE
SHEEP THAN PEOPLE.

NO WORD IN THE DICTIONARY RHYMES WITH
THE WORD ORANGE.

THE NUMBER FOUR IS THE ONLY NUMBER
WITH THE SAME AMOUNT OF LETTERS!

OCTOPUSES HAVE NINE BRAINS.

OLYMPUS MONS IS THE TALLEST PLANETARY
MOUNTAIN IN THE SOLAR SYSTEM. IT IS ALMOST
2.5 TIMES MOUNT EVEREST'S HEIGHT ABOVE SEA LEVEL.

ONLY MALE TOADS ACTUALLY CROAK.

AS WE GET OLDER OUR AVERAGE BODY
TEMPERATURE DECREASES.

AS WE LIE OUR NOSE GETS WARMER!

OVER 1 BILLION HOURS OF YOUTUBE VIDEOS ARE
WATCHED EVERY DAY! THIS IS MORE THAN NETFLIX
AND FACEBOOK VIDEOS COMBINED TOGETHER!

YOU COULD FIT OVER 1 MILLION EARTHS
INSIDE THE SUN.

OWLS CAN'T MOVE THEIR EYEBALLS

PANTHERS ARE NOT ACTUALLY A SEPARATE SPECIES OF CATS. THEY'RE JUST LEOPARDS OR JAGUARS WITH A BLACK COLOR MUTATION.

PEACHES AND NECTARINES ARE ALMOST GENETICALLY IDENTICAL.

PINEAPPLES WERE A STATUS SYMBOL IN 18TH CENTURY ENGLAND!

PROXIMA CENTAURI IS THE CLOSEST STAR
TO THE EARTH.

RUSSIA IS JUST 2 MILES FROM ALASKA.

SCIENTISTS BELIEVE THAT THERE ARE MORE THAN
10 MILLION DIFFERENT KINDS OF LIFE FORMS
ON EARTH.

SEA LIONS CAN ACTUALLY CLAP TO A BEAT.

SEA SPONGES ARE WIDELY CONSIDERED TO BE THE "LEAST EVOLUTIONARILY ADVANCED" ANIMAL ON THE PLANET.

SLOTHS ARE GREAT SWIMMERS AND CAN HOLD THEIR BREATH FOR UP TO 40 MINUTES UNDERWATER!!

SLUGS HAVE FOUR NOSES.

SNAILS TAKE THE LONGEST NAPS - SOME LASTING AS LONG AS THREE YEARS.

SOME FISH COUGH IN ORDER TO CLEAR
THE PARTICLES AND BACTERIA OUT OF THEIR GILLS.

SOME HUMMINGBIRDS CAN WEIGH LESS
THAN A PENNY!

SPAIN, SWEDEN, AND SWITZERLAND REMAINED
NEUTRAL IN WORLD WAR -II AND DID NOT
JOIN ANY SIDE.

SQUID, OCTOPUS, HORSESHOE CRABS
HAVE BLUE BLOOD!!

POTATOES WERE ONCE USED AS CURRENCY
ON THE SOUTH ATLANTIC ISLAND OF
TRISTAN DA CUNHA!!

STRAWBERRIES ARE THE ONLY FRUIT THAT
HAS ITS SEEDS ON THE OUTSIDE.

THE "SIXTH SICK SHEIK'S SIXTH SHEEP'S SICK" IS
BELIEVED TO BE THE TOUGHEST TONGUE TWISTER
IN THE ENGLISH LANGUAGE.

THE ANDES IN SOUTH AMERICA ARE THE LONGEST
MOUNTAIN RANGE IN THE WORLD.

THE BRAIN IS ACTUALLY NOT CAPABLE OF MULTITASKING. WE MAY THINK WE'RE DOING TWO THINGS AT THE SAME TIME, WE'RE ACTUALLY JUST QUICKLY SWITCHING BETWEEN DIFFERENT TASKS.

THE EARLIEST MENU DATES BACK TO THE MID-1700S IN EUROPE TO ACCOMMODATE HIGH-CLASS RESIDENTS DURING DINNER PARTIES.

THE FASTEST RECORDED RAINDROP TRAVELED AT THE SPEED OF 18 MPH!

THE FEMALE HUMMINGBIRD BUILDS THE WORLD'S SMALLEST BIRD'S NEST - ABOUT THE SIZE OF A WALNUT!

THE FESTIVE TRADITION OF THE CHRISTMAS TREE
DATES BACK THOUSANDS OF YEARS TO THE
ROMANS AND ANCIENT EGYPTIANS.

THE FIRST LIVING CREATURES INTENTIONALLY
SENT INTO SPACE WERE FRUIT FLIES!

THE GRAND CANYON IS THE LARGEST CANYON IN THE
WORLD. LOCATED IN ARIZONA, IT HAS AN ELEVATION OF
2,600 FEET AND A LENGTH OF 277 MILES.

THE GREAT RED SPOT OF JUPITER IS A STORM
THAT HAS BEEN RAGING FOR OVER 200 YEARS!

THE HOTTEST DESERT IN THE WORLD IS THE SAHARA, IN AFRICA. THE AVERAGE TEMPERATURE IS AROUND 30°C (86°F), BUT THE HOTTEST TEMPERATURE EVER RECORDED IS 58°C (136.4°F).

THE HUMAN BODY IS MADE UP OF ABOUT 37 TRILLION CELLS.

THE HUMAN BRAIN WILL TRIPLE ITS SIZE IN THE FIRST YEAR OF LIFE.

THE HUMAN NOSE CAN DETECT AND RECOGNIZE THREE TRILLION DIFFERENT SCENTS.

THE MOST EXPENSIVE BOOK EVER PURCHASED WAS SOLD FOR $30.8 MILLION. IT WAS WRITTEN BY LEONARDO DA VINCI AND WAS BOUGHT BY BILL GATES.

THE OPPOSITE SIDES OF THE DICE ALWAYS ADD UP TO SEVEN.

THE PYRAMID OF KHUFU AT GIZA IS THE LARGEST EGYPTIAN PYRAMID AND WEIGHS AS MUCH AS 16 EMPIRE STATE BUILDINGS!

THE QUEEN OF ENGLAND HAS TWO BIRTHDAYS.

THE SHARK IS THE ONLY FISH THAT CAN BLINK WITH BOTH EYES.

THE SMALLEST COUNTRY IN THE WORLD IS VATICAN CITY IN ROME, ITALY. IT'S ONLY ABOUT 109 ACRES.

THE SOLAR SYSTEM FORMED ABOUT 4.6 BILLION YEARS AGO.

THE SUN IS ABOUT 10,000 DEGREES FAHRENHEIT.

WHILE THE SUN APPEARS SUPER CLOSE, IT WOULD TAKE 70,000 YEARS IN OUR FASTEST SPACESHIP TO REACH IT.

THE SUNSET ON MARS IS BLUE.

THE TALLEST BUILDING IN THE WORLD IS THE BURJ KHALIFA IN DUBAI, IT IS 828 METERS TALL WITH 163 FLOORS.

THE UNITED STATES AND CANADA SHARE THE LONGEST BORDER IN THE WORLD. IT SPANS OVER 1,538 MILES!

THE WORLD'S HEAVIEST CARROT GROWN BY CHRISTOPHER QUALLEY IN THE USA WEIGHED 10.7KG (OR 22.44 LB).

THE WORLD'S LONGEST FRENCH FRY IS 34-INCHES LONG.

THE WORLD'S TALLEST MAN WAS ROBERT WADLOW FROM MICHIGAN, AMERICA. HE MEASURED 8 FEET & 2 INCHES (OR 272CM).

THERE ARE 31,557,600 SECONDS IN A YEAR.

THERE ARE A BILLION BACTERIA IN YOUR
MOUTH AT ANY TIME!

THERE ARE MORE STARS IN SPACE
THAN THERE ARE GRAINS OF SAND ON A BEACH.

THERE ARE MORE TVS IN THE
UNITED STATES OF AMERICA THAN THE
NUMBER OF PEOPLE IN THE UK.

THERE ARE MORE THAN 1,000 KINDS OF
BATS IN THE WORLD.

THERE ARE NO MALE OR FEMALE EARTHWORMS. ALL EARTHWORMS HAVE BOTH MALE AND FEMALE PARTS.

THERE IS A TREE CALLED THE IDIOT FRUIT, IT GROWS IN AUSTRALIA'S DAINTREE RAINFOREST

THERE IS NO SOUND IN SPACE!

THERE MAY HAVE BEEN FOUR DIFFERENT ICE AGES, WHERE THE WORLD WAS COMPLETELY COVERED IN ICE, NOT JUST ONE.

THOMAS EDISON DIDN'T ACTUALLY INVENT THE
LIGHTBULB. HE GOT A PATENT FOR THE INVENTION
IN 1880, WARREN DE LA RUE, A BRITISH
ASTRONOMER, CREATED THE FIRST BULB
FORTY YEARS EARLIER.

TOMATOES AND AVOCADOS ARE ACTUALLY FRUITS,
NOT VEGETABLES.

VENUS IS THE ONLY PLANET THAT SPINS CLOCKWISE!

VENUS IS THE HOTTEST PLANET IN THE SOLAR SYSTEM,
WITH TEMPERATURES OF OVER 450 DEGREES CELCIUS.

WATER COVERS 70% OF THE EARTHS SURFACE

WEARING HEADPHONES FOR JUST AN HOUR
COULD INCREASE THE BACTERIA IN YOUR EAR
BY 700 TIMES.

IN THE ANCIENT OLYMPICS, ATHLETES
PERFORMED NAKED!

CAT PEE GLOWS UNDER A BLACK LIGHT!

COCKROACHES HAVE WHITE BLOOD!

THE ANCIENT ROMANS OFTEN USED STALE URINE AS MOUTHWASH!!

ALL CLOWNFISH ARE BORN MALE. THEY HAVE THE ABILITY TO CHANGE THEIR SEX LATER ON AND THAT CHANGE IS IRREVERSIBLE!!

WOMEN'S HEARTS BEAT FASTER THAN MEN'S.

YOU CAN BUY PIECES OF REAL METEORITE
ON EBAY.

YOU CAN NOT TALK AND INHALE OR EXHALE
AT THE SAME TIME.

YOU CAN'T SMELL ANYTHING WHILE ASLEEP!

YOU FART ON AVERAGE 14 TIMES A DAY, EACH
FART TRAVELS FROM YOUR BODY AT 7 MPH.

YOU MIGHT THINK THAT STARS ARE ALL THE SAME, BUT EACH STAR IS A DIFFERENT COLOR DEPENDING ON ITS TEMPERATURE.

YOUR HEART IS ABOUT THE SAME SIZE AS YOUR FIST.

YOUR NOSE AND EARS CONTINUE GROWING FOR YOUR ENTIRE LIFE.

YOUR SKIN IS THE LARGEST BODY ORGAN!

GIANT PANDAS EAT APPROXIMATELY 28 POUNDS
OF BAMBOO A DAY! THAT'S OVER 5 TONS PER YEAR!

THE NOBEL PEACE PRIZE IS NAMED FOR ALFRED NOBEL,
THE INVENTOR OF DYNAMITE.

ONE OF THE INGREDIENTS NEEDED TO MAKE
DYNAMITE IS PEANUTS.

THE LARGEST LIVING ORGANISM IN THE WORLD IS A
FUNGUS. IT IS IN OREGON, COVERING 2,200 ACRES,
AND IS STILL GROWING.

THE LITTLE KNOWN ANGLO-ZANZIBAR WAR OF 1896 IS REGARDED AS THE SHORTEST WAR IN HISTORY, IT LASTED 38 MINUTES.

SOME TUMORS CAN GROW HAIR, TEETH, BONES, EVEN FINGERNAILS.

YOUR BRAIN USES 10 WATTS OF ENERGY TO THINK AND DOES NOT FEEL PAIN.

GLASS BALLS CAN BOUNCE HIGHER THAN RUBBER ONES.

GARLIC BULBS ARE FULL OF VITAMIN C, IRON,
POTASSIUM, MAGNESIUM, ZINC, AND MORE.
IT ALSO HAS 17 AMINO ACIDS.

THE DOUBLE COCONUT PALM PRODUCED THE BIGGEST
SEED IN THE WORLD AT 45 POUNDS.

ACCORDING TO TORI AVEY, COFFEE BECAME A POPULAR
DRINK IN AMERICA AFTER THE BOSTON TEA
PARTY OF 1773: MAKING THE SWITCH FROM
TEA TO COFFEE WAS CONSIDERED A PATRIOTIC DUTY.

POUND CAKE IS SO-CALLED BECAUSE THE RECIPES
ONCE CALLED FOR A POUND OF BUTTER, A POUND OF
SUGAR, A POUND OF EGGS AND A POUND OF FLOUR.

CARROTS WEREN'T ALWAYS ORANGE: THEY WERE ONCE EXCLUSIVELY PURPLE.

GERMAN CHOCOLATE CAKE IS NOT FROM GERMANY. GERMAN IS ACTUALLY THE LAST NAME OF THE MAN WHO INVENTED A FORM OF BAKING CHOCOLATE (SAM GERMAN).

CILANTRO AND CORIANDER ARE CONSIDERED TO BE THE SAME.

SPAM IS A MASH-UP OF THE WORDS "SPICE" AND "HAM"

THE WRIGHT BROTHERS ONLY FLEW TOGETHER ONCE (THOUGH BOTH PILOTED THE PLANES INDIVIDUALLY): ON MAY 25, 1910 THEY TOOK A SIX-MINUTE FLIGHT PILOTED BY ORVILLE WITH WILBUR AS HIS PASSENGER.

REGARDLESS OF THEIR SIZE, NAVAL TRADITION DECLARES SUBMARINES BE CALLED "BOATS" RATHER THAN "SHIPS."

WALT DISNEY STARTED SKETCHING REGULARLY WHEN HE WAS JUST FOUR YEARS OLD.

ABRAHAM LINCOLN LOST FIVE SEPARATE ELECTIONS BEFORE HE BECAME PRESIDENT OF THE U.S!

PABLO PICASSO ENTERED ART SCHOOL
AROUND THE AGE OF 10.

FREDERICK DOUGLASS TAUGHT HIMSELF
TO READ AND WRITE.

THE PICASSO MUSEUM IN BARCELONA, SPAIN
INCLUDES MANY "EARLY WORKS" FROM
HIS CHILDHOOD.

BEFORE EUROPEAN CONTACT (WHICH CAUSED
POPULATIONS TO DIMINISH RAPIDLY) CALIFORNIA
INDIGENOUS TRIBAL GROUPS SPOKE
MORE THAN 200 UNIQUE DIALECTS.

AFTER LANDING IN IRELAND AFTER HER FIRST
SOLO ATLANTIC FLIGHT, A FARMER ASKED
AMELIA EARHART WHERE SHE WAS FROM. WHEN SHE
SAID AMERICA, HE DIDN'T BELIEVE HER!

THE OLYMPICS USED TO AWARD GOLD
MEDALS FOR ART

SOME TORNADOES CAN BE FASTER THAN
FORMULA ONE RACE CARS!

THE WIND IS SILENT UNTIL IT BLOWS
AGAINST SOMETHING.

THERE ARE ICE CAVES IN ICELAND
THAT HAVE HOT SPRINGS.

THE USA GETS OVER 1200
TORNADOES A YEAR.

LIGHTNING CAN, IN FACT, STRIKE TWICE.

YUMA, ARIZONA GETS OVER 4000 HOURS OF
SUNSHINE A YEAR, MAKING IT THE SUNNIEST
PLACE ON EARTH.

THE LEAST SUNNY PLACE ON EARTH IS THE
SOUTH POLE, WHERE THE SUN ONLY SHINES
FOR 182 DAYS A YEAR.

RAIN CONTAINS VITAMIN B12.

A HURRICANE RELEASES ENOUGH ENERGY IN
ONE SECOND TO EQUAL THAT OF 10 ATOMIC BOMBS.

IT CAN BE TOO WARM TO SNOW, BUT NEVER TOO COLD.

TROPICAL STORMS AND HURRICANES
STARTED GETTING "NAMED" IN 1953.

WORMS WIGGLE UP FROM THE GROUND
WHEN A FLOOD IS COMING.

THE MOON IS VERY HOT (224 DEGREES
FAHRENHEIT, AVERAGE) DURING THE DAY BUT VERY
COLD (-243 DEGREES AVERAGE) AT NIGHT.

ONE TEASPOON OF A NEUTRON STAR WOULD WEIGH
SIX BILLION TONS.

SALLY RIDE WAS THE FIRST AMERICAN WOMAN
TO GO INTO SPACE, ON JUNE 18, 1983.

EVEN IN AN AIRPLANE, A TRIP TO PLUTO WOULD
TAKE ABOUT 800 YEARS.

NEPTUNE'S DAYS ARE 16 HOURS LONG.

THE EARTH'S CORE IS AS HOT AS THE
SURFACE OF THE SUN.

IN 2011, TEN-YEAR-OLD KATHRYN GRAY DISCOVERED A SUPERNOVA THAT NO ONE ELSE HAD SEEN BEFORE.

IN THE CARIBBEAN THERE ARE OYSTERS THAT CAN CLIMB TREES.

SATURN'S RINGS ARE MADE FROM TRILLIONS OF CHUNKS OF ORBITING ICE.

ALPHA CENTAURI ISN'T A STAR, BUT A STAR SYSTEM. IT IS 4.22 LIGHT-YEARS AWAY.

IN A NORMAL LIFETIME, AN AMERICAN WILL EAT
200 LBS OF PEANUTS AND 10,000 LBS OF MEAT.

EUROPA, ONE OF JUPITER'S MOONS, HAS SALTWATER
GEYSERS THAT ARE 20X TALLER THAN MT. EVEREST.

THE HIEROGLYPH FOR 100,000 IS A TADPOLE.

MOSQUITOES PREFER CHILDREN TO ADULTS AND
BLONDES TO BRUNETTES.

MEXICO CITY IS THE OLDEST CAPITAL CITY
IN THE AMERICAS.

EARLY MERMAID SIGHTINGS CAN BE ATTRIBUTED TO
DEHYDRATION AND MANATEES.

SLOTHS CANNOT SHIVER TO STAY WARM, SO HAVE
DIFFICULTY MAINTAINING THEIR BODY
TEMPERATURE ON RAINY DAYS.

IN THE WILD, SOME REINDEER TRAVEL MORE THAN
3000 MILES IN A SINGLE YEAR.

OTHER THAN HUMANS, EMPEROR PENGUINS ARE
THE ONLY WARM-BLOODED ANIMAL TO STAY
ON ANTARCTICA FOR THE WINTER.

THE BIGGEST FOSSIL OF A SPIDER WAS FOUND
IN CHINA. IT IS ONE-INCH LONG AND
165 MILLION YEARS OLD.

THE LARGEST LIVING ANIMAL IS THE BLUE WHALE,
WHICH CAN MEASURE AS MUCH AS 100 FEET.

IN THE WINTERTIME, REINDEER GROW THEIR FACIAL
HAIR LONG ENOUGH TO COVER THEIR MOUTHS,
WHICH PROTECTS THEIR MUZZLES
WHEN GRAZING IN THE SNOW.

DOLPHINS OFTEN WRAP SEA SPONGES AROUND THEIR LONG SNOUTS TO PROTECT THEM FROM CUTS WHILE FORAGING FOR FOOD.

DOGS HAVE WET NOSES BECAUSE THEY SECRETE A THIN LAYER OF MUCUS, WHICH ACTUALLY HELPS DOGS SMELL!

THE LARGEST LAND ANIMAL IN ANTARCTICA IS AN INSECT: THE COLUMBOLA. PENGUINS ARE CONSIDERED MARINE ANIMALS.

THERE ARE 222 OWL SPECIES IN THE WORLD. MOST ARE NOCTURNAL, BUT A FEW ARE ACTIVE DURING THE DAYTIME, SUCH AS THE BARRED OWL.

SHARKS DON'T HUNT HUMANS OR CONSIDER THEM FOOD. SHARKS INCIDENTS OCCUR WHEN SHARKS HUNT FOR SEALS, DOLPHINS OR OTHER "HUMAN-SIZED" PREY.

IN 1962, WILT CHAMBERLAIN SCORED 100 POINTS IN A SINGLE NBA BASKETBALL GAME. NO ONE HAS BROKEN THIS RECORD.

BABE RUTH BEGAN HIS CAREER AS A PITCHER: RUTH WAS BOTH A LEFT-HANDED PITCHER AND LEFT-HANDED BATTER.

THE MOST MEDALS WON FOR OLYMPIC BASKETBALL (MALE OR FEMALE) ARE BOTH HELD BY WOMEN: TERESA EDWARDS AND LISA LESLIE WITH FOUR GOLD MEDALS EACH.

WILMA RUDOLPH (WHO SET THE WORLD RECORD IN 1960 FOR 100, 200 & 4X100-METER RELAY) HAD POLIO, SCARLET FEVER AND PNEUMONIA AS A CHILD, LEADING DOCTORS TO BELIEVE SHE'D NEVER WALK AGAIN.

SUPER BOWL REFEREES ALSO GET SUPER BOWL RINGS.

IN 1919, CLEVELAND INDIANS PITCHER RAY CALDWELL WAS STRUCK BY LIGHTNING IN THE MIDDLE OF THE 9TH INNING. HE KEPT PLAYING!

THE 'G' ON THE GREEN BAY PACKERS HELMET STANDS FOR "GREATNESS" NOT GREEN BAY!

BASEBALLS LAST AN AVERAGE
OF SEVEN PITCHES.

MANON RHEAUME IS THE ONLY WOMAN
TO HAVE PLAYED IN AN NHL GAME.

GOLF IS HAS BEEN PLAYED ON THE MOON. IN 1971,
ALAN SHEPARD HIT A BALL WHILE ON THE MOON
AS PART OF THE APOLLO 14 MISSION.

THE SHORTEST PLAYER IN THE NATIONAL HOCKEY
LEAGUE (NHL) WAS GOALTENDER ROY WOTERS WHO
MEASURED 5 FT. 3 IN. TALL.

ONE-QUARTER OF YOUR BONES
ARE IN YOUR FEET.

HUMAN TEETH ARE AS STRONG
AS SHARK TEETH!

THE AVERAGE BRAIN WEIGHS ABOUT THREE POUNDS.
A NEWBORN BRAIN WEIGHS ABOUT
3/4 OF A POUND.

THERE ARE ABOUT 100,000 MUSCLES IN AN
ELEPHANT'S TRUNK, BUT NOT A SINGLE BONE.

PRAIRIE DOGS "KISS" EACH OTHER AS A WAY
TO IDENTIFY EACH OTHER.

FEMALE LIONS DO ABOUT 90% OF
THE HUNTING.

COWS GET STRESSED WHEN THEY ARE
SEPARATED FROM THEIR BEST FRIENDS.

THERE ARE OVER 400 MILLION DOGS
IN THE ENTIRE WORLD.

ORCAS ARE NOT WHALES AT ALL, THEY ARE
ACTUALLY A TYPE OF DOLPHIN.

CATS ONLY MEOW TO TALK TO HUMANS.
THEY DO NOT MEOW TO COMMUNICATE
WITH OTHER CATS.

BABY ELEPHANTS USE THEIR TRUNKS THE SAME
WAY THAT BABY HUMANS USE A PACIFIER.
BABY ELEPHANTS FIND SUCKING ON
THEIR TRUNKS VERY CALMING.

COWS HAVE 4 STOMACHS.

RATS ARE TICKLISH!
THEY LAUGH WHEN THEY ARE TICKLED.

MALE SEAHORSES ARE THE
ONES WHO GIVE BIRTH.

THE AVERAGE CHOCOLATE BAR HAS
8 INSECT LEGS IN IT.

BATS CAN EAT UP TO 1,000
INSECTS IN AN HOUR.

POLAR BEARS ARE NOT WHITE
THEIR FUR IS ACTUALLY TRANSPARENT.

FLAMINGOS EAT WITH THEIR
HEAD UPSIDE DOWN.

BATS ARE THE ONLY MAMMALS THAT CAN FLY,
BUT THEIR LEG BONES ARE SO THIN THAT IT IS ALMOST
IMPOSSIBLE FOR THEM TO WALK.

A GROUP OF OWLS IS CALLED
A PARLIAMENT.

ANTS DON'T HAVE LUNGS.

GRIZZLY BEARS CAN RUN UP
TO 30 MILES PER HOUR.

AFTER HUMANS, MOSQUITOES ARE THE DEADLIEST
ANIMAL ON EARTH.

NEW WORMS ARE NOT BORN. THEY HATCH FROM
COCOONS SMALLER THAN A GRAIN OF RICE.

STARFISH HAVE NO BRAINS.

ALASKA IS BOTH THE MOST WESTERN AND MOST EASTERN STATE IN THE UNITED STATES.

GREENLAND IS THE WORLD'S LARGEST ISLAND.

THE ENGLISH LANGUAGE IS SPOKEN IN MORE THAN 100 COUNTRIES AROUND THE WORLD.

ANTARCTICA IS THE ONLY CONTINENT WITH
NO PERMANENT HUMAN RESIDENTS.

DUST FROM THE SAHARA DESERT IN AFRICA CAN
TRAVEL HUGE DISTANCES.
IT CAN REACH AS FAR AS TEXAS.

MAINE IS THE CLOSEST STATE TO AFRICA.

THE STATE OF CALIFORNIA HAS MORE PEOPLE
THAN THE ENTIRE COUNTRY OF CANADA.

THE DEAD SEA IS THE LOWEST
PLACE ON THE PLANET.

ISTANBUL IS THE ONLY CITY IN THE WORLD
LOCATED ON TWO CONTINENTS...
EUROPE AND ASIA.

THE ATLANTIC OCEAN IS SALTIER THAN
THE PACIFIC OCEAN.

PEOPLE CAN FART AFTER THEY DIE.

CLOUDS AREN'T WEIGHTLESS
THEY CAN ACTUALLY BE WAY OVER
A MILLION POUNDS.

BECAUSE BANANAS CONTAIN POTASSIUM,
THEY ARE ACTUALLY RADIOACTIVE.

CHALK IS MADE UP OF FOSSILS.

THE ACID IN YOUR STOMACH CAN
DISSOLVE STEEL.

ALL PLANETS SPIN COUNTERCLOCKWISE
EXCEPT FOR VENUS.

PLANKTON, SEAWEED, AND OTHER OCEAN ORGANISMS
CREATE OVER HALF THE WORLD'S OXYGEN.

BEES HAVE 5 EYES. THERE ARE 3 SMALL EYES ON
THE TOP OF A BEE'S HEAD AND 2 LARGER
ONES IN FRONT.

HUMANS LOSE ABOUT 50-100
HAIRS A DAY.

BOYS HAVE FEWER TASTE BUDS
THAN GIRLS.

A SOCCER BALL IS MADE UP OF 32 LEATHER PANELS,
HELD TOGETHER BY 642 STITCHES.

IT TAKES YOUR BODY ABOUT 12 HOURS
TO FULLY DIGEST FOOD.

ALEXANDER THE GREAT WAS BURIED ALIVE.

CLEOPATRA WASN'T EGYPTIAN
SHE WAS GREEK.

THE STATUE OF LIBERTY WAS ORIGINALLY
SUPPOSED TO BE LOCATED IN THE SUEZ CANAL.

TUG OF WAR USED TO BE AN
OLYMPIC SPORT.

DURING THE VICTORIAN ERA, IT WAS POPULAR FOR
PEOPLE TO TAKE PHOTOGRAPHS OF THEIR
LOVED ONES AFTER THEY HAD DIED.

THOMAS EDISON AND JOHN ADAMS DIED
HOURS APART ON JULY 4, 1826.

THE WAR BETWEEN THE NETHERLANDS AND THE
ISLES OF SCILLY LASTED 335 YEARS,
NOT A SINGLE PERSON WAS KILLED.

BEFORE ALARM CLOCKS, PEOPLE WOULD PAY SOMEONE
TO KNOCK ON THEIR WINDOW AND WAKE THEM UP.
THEY WERE CALLED KNOCKER-UPPERS.

ALL BRITISH ARMORED VEHICLES HAVE THE
EQUIPMENT NEEDED TO MAKE TEA.

ARITHMOPHOBIA IS THE FEAR
OF NUMBERS.

IN YOUR LIFETIME, YOU WILL SPEND
25 YEARS JUST SLEEPING.

BROWN IS THE MOST COMMON EYE COLOR.

YOU WILL GET CELL PHONE SERVICE ON
THE TOP OF MOUNT EVEREST.

NEWBORN BABIES ARE COLORBLIND.

THE COLORS OF A RAINBOW ALWAYS
APPEAR IN THE SAME ORDER.

BLUE, RED, AND YELLOW ARE PRIMARY COLORS
THESE COLORS PLUS WHITE AND BLACK BLEND
TO MAKE ALL OTHER COLORS.

RED IS THE FIRST COLOR A BABY CAN SEE.

WHITE IS THE MOST POPULAR CAR COLOR.

A BLUE WHALE'S TONGUE IS HEAVIER
THAN AN ELEPHANT.

A CRAB'S TASTE BUDS ARE
ON ITS FEET.

AN OCTOPUS HAS THREE HEARTS.

AMERICAN LOBSTERS CAN LIVE
TO BE 20 YEARS OLD.

NO TWO SPOT PATTERNS ON A WHALE SHARK
ARE THE SAME, THEY ARE AS UNIQUE
AS FINGERPRINTS.

THE UNITED STATES HAS THE FOURTH-LONGEST
WATER SYSTEM IN THE WORLD.

THE TALLEST MONUMENT IN THE UNITED STATES
IS THE GATEWAY ARCH IN ST. LOUIS.

KANSAS CITY, MISSOURI, HAS MORE FOUNTAINS
THAN ANY OTHER CITY IN THE WORLD
BESIDES ROME.

TENNESSEE AND MISSOURI EACH SHARE
BORDERS WITH EIGHT STATES.

AB NEGATIVE IS THE RAREST BLOOD TYPE.

THE STRONGEST MUSCLE IN THE BODY
IS THE JAW.

THE AVERAGE TONGUE IS ABOUT
THREE INCHES LONG.

POTATOES WERE THE FIRST VEGETABLE TO
BE GROWN IN SPACE.

BANANAS ARE TECHNICALLY HERBS.

THE DINOSAUR WITH THE LONGEST NAME IS
MICROPACHYCEPHALOSAURUS.

A NIGERSAURUS HAS AN UNUSUAL SKULL CONTAINING AS MANY AS 500 SLENDER TEETH.

OVER 700 DINOSAURS HAVE BEEN IDENTIFIED AND NAMED, HOWEVER, SCIENTISTS BELIEVE THERE ARE MANY MORE TO BE DISCOVERED.

SNAKES, CROCODILES AND BEES WERE JUST A FEW OF THE ANIMALS WHO LIVED ALONGSIDE DINOSAURS.

GEORGE WASHINGTON, THOMAS JEFFERSON, THEODORE ROOSEVELT AND ABRAHAM LINCOLN ARE THE FOUR PRESIDENTS ON MOUNT RUSHMORE.

THE WASHINGTON MONUMENT IS THE TALLEST
UNREINFORCED STONE MASONRY
STRUCTURE IN THE WORLD.

PRESIDENT THEODORE ROOSEVELT IS RESPONSIBLE
FOR GIVING THE WHITE HOUSE ITS NAME.

ELVIS PRESLEY WAS ONE OF THE LARGEST PRIVATE
DONORS TO THE PEARL HARBOR MEMORIAL.

THE LONGEST TENNIS MATCH LASTED 11 HOURS AND
FIVE MINUTES AT WIMBLEDON IN 2010.

WOMEN FIRST COMPETED IN THE OLYMPIC
GAMES IN 1900 IN PARIS.

WRESTLING WAS THE WORLD'S FIRST SPORT.

THE FIFA WORLD CUP (SOCCER) IS ONE OF THE MOST
VIEWED SPORTING EVENTS ON TELEVISION.

THE EMPIRE STATE BUILDING GETS STRUCK BY
LIGHTNING AN AVERAGE OF 25 TIMES A YEAR.

IN 1899, IT WAS SO COLD THAT THE
MISSISSIPPI RIVER FROZE.

IN THE AVERAGE LIFETIME, A PERSON WILL WALK THE
EQUIVALENT OF 5 TIMES AROUND THE EQUATOR.

HURRICANES NORTH OF THE EARTH'S EQUATOR
SPIN COUNTERCLOCKWISE.

HURRICANES SOUTH OF THE EARTH'S EQUATOR
SPIN CLOCKWISE.

ABRAHAM LINCOLN STOOD AT 6 FEET 4 INCHES MAKING HIM ONE OF THE TALLEST PRESIDENTS.

FORMER U.S PRESIDENT BILL CLINTON HAS TWO GRAMMY AWARDS.

THE SHORTEST-SERVING PRESIDENT WAS WILLIAM HENRY HARRISON, HE WAS THE NINT PRESIDENT OF THE UNITED STATES FOR 31 DAYS IN 1841.

FRANKLIN D. ROOSEVELT IS THE ONLY AMERICAN PRESIDENT TO HAVE SERVED MORE THAN TWO TERMS.

TIGER ROARS WERE USED FOR THE LION KING,
AS LIONS WEREN'T LOUD ENOUGH.

WALT DISNEY WORLD RESORT IS ABOUT THE SAME
SIZE AS SAN FRANCISCO.

MICKEY MOUSE WAS THE FIRST ANIMATED CHARACTER
TO RECEIVE A STAR ON THE HOLLYWOOD
WALK OF FAME.

POCAHONTAS IS THE ONLY DISNEY PRINCESS
WITH A TATTOO.

DISNEY'S BEAUTY AND THE BEAST WAS THE
FIRST ANIMATED FILM IN HISTORY TO BE NOMINATED
FOR BEST PICTURE AT THE OSCARS.

EARS OF CORN GENERALLY HAVE AN EVEN
NUMBER OF ROWS.

ALTHOUGH FROOT LOOPS CEREAL SIGNATURE "O'S"
COME IN MANY COLORS, THEY'RE ALL THE
SAME FLAVOR.

THE CAESAR SALAD WAS BORN IN TIJUANA, MEXICO.

ONE OUT OF EVERY FOUR HAZELNUTS ON
THE PLANET MAKES ITS WAY INTO A
JAR OF NUTELLA.

THE "GUINNESS BOOK OF WORLD RECORDS" WAS
FIRST PUBLISHED IN 1955.

THE SIMPSONS IS THE LONGEST-RUNNING ANIMATED
TELEVISION SHOW (BASED ON EPISODES).

THE WORLD'S LARGEST WEDDING CAKE
WEIGHED 15,032 POUNDS.

ASHRITA FURMAN IS THE PERSON WITH THE MOST GUINNESS WORLD RECORDS TITLES.

THE LARGEST GATHERING OF PEOPLE DRESSED AS SUPERMAN WAS 867, ACHIEVED BY A GROUP IN THE U.K.

WHEN DINOSAURS EXISTED, THERE USED TO BE VOLCANOES THAT WERE ERUPTING ON THE MOON.

IF A POLAR BEAR AND A GRIZZLY BEAR MATE, THEIR OFFSPRING IS CALLED A "PIZZY BEAR".

A SINGLE STRAND OF SPAGHETTI IS
CALLED A "SPAGHETTO".

IF YOU CUT DOWN A CACTUS IN ARIZONA, YOU'LL BE
PENALIZED FOR UP TO 25 YEARS IN JAIL.

SOUR PATCH KIDS ARE FROM THE SAME MANUFACTURER
AS SWEDISH FISH. THE RED SOUR PATCH KIDS ARE
THE SAME CANDY AS SWEDISH FISH, BUT WITH
SOUR SUGAR.

ICELAND DOES NOT HAVE A RAILWAY SYSTEM.

THE TONGUE IS THE ONLY MUSCLE IN YOUR BODY
THAT IS ATTACHED FROM ONE END.

THE ROMAN - PERSIAN WARS ARE THE LONGEST IN
HISTORY, LASTING OVER 680 YEARS. THEY BEGAN
IN 54 BC AND ENDED IN 628 AD.

AT BIRTH, A BABY PANDA IS SMALLER
THAN A MOUSE.

THE VOICE ACTOR OF SPONGEBOB AND THE VOICE
ACTOR OF KAREN, PLANKTON'S COMPUTER WIFE, HAVE
BEEN MARRIED SINCE 1995.

THE HUMAN EYE IS SO SENSITIVE THAT, IF THE
EARTH WERE FLAT AND IT WAS A DARK NIGHT,
A CANDLE'S FLAME COULD BE SEEN
FROM 30 MILES AWAY.

THE COLOR RED DOESN'T REALLY MAKE BULLS
ANGRY; THEY ARE COLOR-BLIND.

65% OF AUTISTIC PEOPLE ARE LEFT-HANDED, AND
ONLY 10% OF PEOPLE, IN GENERAL, ARE
LEFT-HANDED.

IN 2007, SCOTLAND SPENT $125,000 ON A NEW
NATIONAL SLOGAN. THE WINNING ENTRY WAS:
"WELCOME TO SCOTLAND".

UNTIL 2016, THE "HAPPY BIRTHDAY" SONG WAS NOT FOR PUBLIC USE. MEANING, PRIOR TO 2016, IT WAS COPYRIGHTED AND YOU HAD TO PAY A LICENSE TO USE IT.

WHEN MICE LIVE IN THE WILD, THEY TYPICALLY ONLY LIVE FOR ABOUT SIX MONTHS.

LETTUCE IS A MEMBER OF THE SUNFLOWER FAMILY.

SAINT LUCIA IS THE ONLY COUNTRY IN THE WORLD NAMED AFTER A WOMAN.

THERE IS A TOWN IN NEBRASKA CALLED MONOWI
WITH A POPULATION OF ONE. THE ONLY
RESIDENT IS A WOMAN WHO IS THE MAYOR,
BARTENDER, AND LIBRARIAN.

VENUS AND MERCURY ARE THE ONLY TWO PLANETS
IN OUR SOLAR SYSTEM THAT DO NOT
HAVE A MOON.

AUGUSTUS CAESAR WAS THE WEALTHIEST MAN
TO EVER LIVE IN HISTORY.

SCOTLAND WAS ONE OF THE FEW COUNTRIES ABLE
TO HOLD OFF BEING CONQUERED BY THE ROMANS
IN THE FIRST CENTURY A.D.

THE UNIQUE SMELL OF RAIN ACTUALLY COMES FROM PLANT OILS, BACTERIA, AND OZONE.

ONLY PRIMATES, HUMANS, AND OPOSSUMS HAVE OPPOSABLE THUMBS.

TIC TACS GOT THEIR NAME FROM THE SOUND THEY MAKE WHEN THEY ARE TOSSED AROUND IN THEIR CONTAINER.

THERE IS A VILLAGE IN RUSSIA CALLED TSOVKRA WHERE EVERY RESIDENT CAN TIGHTROPE WALK.

NILE CROCODILES HAVE BEEN FOUND IN FLORIDA. THEY ARE THE SECOND-LARGEST CROC AND MORE DANGEROUS THAN THE NATIVE CROCODILES AND ALLIGATORS IN FLORIDA.

EVEN THOUGH IRISH IS THE OFFICIAL LANGUAGE OF IRELAND, POLISH IS MORE WIDELY SPOKEN.

IN JAPAN, DOMINO'S STARTED TESTING PIZZA DELIVERY VIA REINDEER IN 2016.

BEES ACTUALLY HAVE KNEES.

SANTA CLAUS WAS ISSUED A PILOT'S LICENSE FROM
THE U.S. GOVERNMENT IN 1927. THEY ALSO GAVE
HIM AIRWAY MAPS AND PROMISED TO KEEP
THE RUNWAY LIGHTS ON.

THE DANGLY THING IN THE BACK OF YOUR THROAT
IS CALLED A UVULA.

A CAT HAS 32 MUSCLES IN EACH EAR.

A KITCHEN SINK CONTAINS MORE
BACTERIA THAN A TOILET.

THE MEMBRANES IN YOUR NASAL PASSAGES CAN PRODUCE UP TO SEVEN LITERS OF SNOT A WEEK!

HUMANS FART ENOUGH GAS IN A DAY TO FILL A PARTY BALLOON!

YOU LOSE THE ENTIRE OUTER LAYER OF YOUR SKIN IN THE SPACE OF ABOUT TWO TO FOUR WEEKS.

CELLPHONES CAN CARRY TEN TIMES MORE BACTERIA THAN TOILET SEATS!

ROMANS USED POWDERED MOUSE BRAINS
AS TOOTHPASTE

IF YOU DON'T PUT THE TOILET SEAT DOWN WHEN
YOU FLUSH, INVISIBLE GERMS CAN BE SENT FLYING
AS FAR AS SIX FEET AWAY.

THE 'FIVE-SECOND RULE' DOES NOT EXIST! BACTERIA
DOES NOT WAIT TO CONTAMINATE YOUR FOOD.

THE CORPSE FLOWER LITERALLY SMELLS
LIKE ROTTING FLESH.

BLONDE PEOPLE HAVE MORE HAIR
THAN DARK-HAIRED PEOPLE.

NEPAL IS THE ONLY COUNTRY THAT HAS A NON-
RECTANGULAR FLAG. IT IS ALSO ASYMMETRICAL.

UNLIKE MOST CATS, TIGERS LOVE THE WATER
AND CAN EASILY SWIM THREE OR FOUR MILES.

IN 1510, A TRIAL WAS HELD IN FRANCE TO DETERMINE
THE GUILT OF A GROUP OF RATS ACCUSED
OF STEALING BARLEY.

THE FIRST CITY IN THE WORLD TO HAVE A
POPULATION OF MORE THAN ONE MILLION
WAS ROME.

SNAKES CAN SEE THROUGH THEIR TRANSPARENT
EYELIDS WHEN THEY ARE CLOSED.

THE STATUE OF LIBERTY WEIGHS 225 TONS.

ON AVERAGE, RIGHT-HANDED PEOPLE LIVE 9 YEARS
LONGER THAN THEIR LEFT-HANDED
COUNTERPARTS.

ON AVERAGE, AMERICANS EAT 18 ACRES
OF PIZZA EVERY DAY.

ALMONDS AND PISTACHIOS ARE THE ONLY
NUTS MENTIONED IN THE BIBLE.

DINOSAURS DID NOT EAT GRASS: THERE WASN'T
ANY AT THAT TIME.

CHOCOLATE WAS INTRODUCED INTO THE USA IN 1765
WHEN COCOA BEANS WERE BROUGHT FROM
THE WEST INDIES TO DORCHESTER, MASSACHUSETTS.

IN 1934, A GUST OF WIND REACHED 371 KM/H ON MOUNT WASHINGTON IN NEW HAMPSHIRE, USA.

MOSQUITOES HAVE 47 TEETH.

THE LARGEST GREAT WHITE SHARK EVER CAUGHT MEASURED 37 FEET. IT WAS FOUND IN NEW BRUNSWICK IN 1930.

AUSTRALIA IS THE ONLY COUNTRY THAT IS ALSO A CONTINENT.

SEVEN PERCENT OF AMERICANS CLAIM
THEY NEVER BATHE AT ALL.

THE PANCREAS PRODUCES INSULIN.

STARFISH HAVE FIVE EYES - ONE AT THE END OF
EACH LEG. SOME HAVE UP TO 20 LEGS/EYES!

A NEWBORN KANGAROO IS ONLY ABOUT
1 INCH IN LENGTH.

THE PENTAGON IN WASHINGTON, D.C. HAS FIVE SIDES, FIVE STORIES, AND FIVE ACRES IN THE MIDDLE.

STARFISH DON'T HAVE BRAINS.

SNAKES ARE TRUE CARNIVORES AS THEY EAT NOTHING BUT OTHER ANIMALS.

PORCUPINES FLOAT IN WATER.

BECAUSE OF THE ROTATION OF THE EARTH, AN
OBJECT CAN BE THROWN FARTHER IF
IT IS THROWN WEST.

———————————————————

AMAZE YOUR FRIENDS AND FAMILY WITH ALL THIS
NEW & USELESS KNOWLEDGE.

SCAN THIS CODE TO GET SOME FREE
KID-FRIENDLY ACTIVITIES!

Made in the USA
Middletown, DE
17 August 2022

71656788R00073